LIFE'S
UNEXPECTED
WAYS

Elena Belias

PublishAmerica
Baltimore

ISBN: 1-4241-1653-8
PUBLISHED BY PUBLISHAMERICA, LLLP
www.publishamerica.com
Baltimore

Printed in the United States of America

LIFE'S
UNEXPECTED
WAYS

A New

Saying Goodbye
Is Not Easy
Don't Ask Why
It Makes You Queasy

Closing Old Doors
New Beginnings
Will Bring You More
What's In It For Me

"A New"
Start At Other Places
Will Bring You More
New Faces
Open More Doors

At Times Heals Your Soul
Makes You Cry
Just Let Go Of The Old
I Won't Lie

May Be What You Need
Look At All The New Things
Just have to Believe
What Life Can Bring

Another

Another Day
Another Night
Not going my way
Just isn't right
Got to be another way
Tired of these games
You know what to say
Your so lame
Another day
Another night
What can I say
Just isn't right
Never going be the same
Set me Free
Tired of these Games
Just not for Me
Another Way
Seems to Be
Another way
Got to Be Free

Broken Promises

Broken promises
Is what you've given me
With those kisses
Don't think I can't see

What you're doing to me
Playing your games
Broken promises
Don't think I can't see

Making me believe
You really want me
I was so stupid ,
Now I see

Broken promises
That's all you leave
Only Sweet Dreams
Wanting only one thing from me

No more dreams
Broken promises
Only hot steamy
Left over kisses

Is what you'll be missing
Just can't believe
All that kissing
Was just a dream

Change

Everything Started Changing
The Day You Left Me
Now I'm Starting To Believe
Never Thought I'd Be Free

It's Easy To See
It's Only For The Better
Change Is What I Need
Never Say Never

Today Is Another Day
You Gave Me Back My Dignity
Believe In What I Say
This Is What I Need

The Day You Left Me
Things Started To Change
Never Thought I'd Feel So Free
Not Looking For Blame

Gave Me Back My Dignity
The Day You Left
It's Just What I Need
Enough Said

No More Crying
Feel Stronger Than Ever Been
Don't Feel Like Dying
Change Is What I Need

Dearest Friend

For Those Who've Passed On

You were an Aunt
You were a Friend
You were a Sister
You were a Mother
Can't Believe it
Now Your Gone
One that Everyone Depended On
Always Being A Friend
Loved By Many
Thoughtful and Kind
You'll Be In Our Hearts and Minds
It's So Sad to See You Go
You'll Be Missed
By So Many
Nephews and Nieces
Family and Friends
NOW YOUR GONE
WE'LL MISS YOU
MAY YOU REST IN PEACE
OUR DEAREST FRIEND

Doesn't Matter

Doesn't matter
What I feel
Makes me sadder
Knowing it's not real

You'll never know
How I really feel
Never did show
Me the real deal

Playing with my heart
Is all you've done
Broke it apart
Nothing but this song

Nothing but a heartbreaker
With the blues
Always a taker
It's what you do

Take what you want
I'll be gone
Doesn't matter
It's all done

"Doesn't matter"
What I feel for you
What you say
Nothing you can do
There is no way

For a While

Maybe you're just what I need
Even if it's for awhile
Oh can't you see
Let's do that extra mile

Life isn't what we expect
Like throwing a dice
That you can bet
It's apart of life

We're all just learning
All about give and take
We all have a yearning
Even if it's a mistake

It isn't always what it seems
Not always what we expect
With broken dreams
We learn to accept

You're what I need
Even for a little while
You just don't see
You drive me wild

For So Long

You looking at me
Me looking at you
For so long
I've had this crush

When you smile
Just one look
You light up my life
That's all it took

Wish this crush
So sweet so kind
You make me blush
Always on my mind

For so long
Who would have known
Would be a lot more
It started to show

Every time you come by
Makes me feel like dancing
I feel so shy
Just can't see

Shivers down my spine
Oh I never
Felt so alive
Hope it lasts forever

He's Gone
Those Who Have Passed

He's GoneCan't Believe it's So
You Died So Tragically
To Fast To Soon

Wish You Were Still Here
Loved By Many
Yet It's Unfair

A Brother
An Uncle
A Son
And A Friend

Can't Believe Your Gone
You'll Be Remembered
Till The End Of Time
Always On Our Minds

He's Gone
Our Dearest Friend
May You Rest In Peace
We'll Miss You

Hidden Secrets

Hidden secrets we all hide
Even things we dream
Till the day we die
Something you can't believe

Hidden secrets
Just look and see
The way they treating you
It just couldn't be

Think we won't know
You may lie
In time it will all show
Thinking you'll get by

Hidden secrets
All through life
These things will eat you
Some are not very nice

We know there not right
Hidden Secrets
They happen every night
Even when they smile and greet you

In Life

People In Life
Can Be So Cruel
Not Very Nice
They Take You For A Fool

"In Life"
Not Everyone Is Your Friend
Those Who Are Cruel
You'll Find Out In The End
Use You As Their Tool

But It's Up To You
Whether You'd Be Their Fool
When You Find Things They Do
They're Not So Cool

Don't want to be used
Could Never Be Your Fool
They Will Abuse
Be So Cruel

"In Life"
You Can Be Free
It's Up To You
Take It From Me
What You Want to Do

Inside

The first I laid eyes one you
Just like in my dream
It was like I knew
What you were going to do

All that chemistry
Looking into those eyes
Was the best thing for me
Oh how much I tried

Just could not deny
Those feeling inside
Didn't know why
Something I can't hide

"Inside"
You send shivers down my spine
Sure feels like love
Can't you see it in my eyes
Makes me want you more

If only you knew
Trying to hide
I'm crazy for you
Keeping it inside

Isn't It

Isn't it wonderful
Isn't it strange
Life is never dull
There's always change

Great feeling inside
What's on my mind
Don't want to hide
No need to lie

Got you in my life
Isn't it wonderful
Isn't it nice
Never dull

No need for me to cry
Saying what's on my mind
No reason to lie
It'll be just fine

Isn't it strange
So many places
How life changes
So many places

Isn't What It Seems

Life Isn't Always
What It Seems
People Never Say
What They Mean

Just When You Think
You Have Everything
Within A Blink
You Have Nothing

Take Away Your Dream
That's When You Find
All What Life Means
People Aren't So Kind

Isn't What It Seems
Don't Let Them Bring You Down
Never Give Up Your Dreams
They Want to See you Frown

Life Isn't Always What It Seems
People Pretend To Be Your Friend
They Take What They Need
Till The Very End

Isn't What It Seems
That's When You Find
You've Lost Your Dream
Even Losing Your Mind

It's Happening

Can't believe this is happening
Feels just like a dream
This feeling of being happy
Is it what it seems

You only appear in my dreams
Can't believe
Now your real
Don't have to sleep

Can't believe it's true
Just your touch
Things you do
So much love

It's happening
Just like in my dream
Now I'm laughing
This really has to be

It's happening
So many things
Now I'm so happy
Look what life brings

Can't believe this is happening
Thought it only happens in dreams
Can't believe I'm singing
Can't believe what I'm seeing

It's Time

Don't you think it's time
We make it right
We're no good as lovers
Better off as friends

"It's Time"
To make up our minds
Have to make that move
Stop wasting my time
You know what to do
Have to get you out of my mind
Get you out of my life
Your no longer mine
Your cold as ice

"It's Time"
To make a new
No more wasting time
To do the things I can do
Have to go on with my life

It's just what I 'm going to do
No longer mine
Getting rid of you
Made up my mind

I've Told You

How Many Times
Have I Told You
Love Doesn't Last
Get It Out Of Your Mind

When You Live In The Past
Can Be So Sad
Things Go So Fast
Got To Be Glad

For What You Have
Now In Your Life
Don't Be Mad
Things Could Be Nice

"I've Told You"
Let Go Of The Past
Be Glad For What You Have
For Things Don't Last
Hold On To Love

Something So Rare
You'll Never Know
Till You Care
Or It'll Be Gone

Lazy Crazy Man

Lazy Crazy Man
You Even Eat Out Of A Can
Look You Fool
Your Even Starting To Drool

Lazy Crazy Man
Can't Even Give Me A Hand
Lazy Crazy Man
Just Want to Lay In The Sand
Lazy Crazy Man

All You Do Is Watch TV
Never Let Me Be
Think Everything In Life Is Free
You Need To Join The Army

You Think You're So Fine
Driving Me Out Of My Mind
Don't Even Know How To Be Kind
Lazy Crazy Man

Letting Go

Don't You Know
You've Got To Believe
Letting Go
You'll Achieve

Don't Hold On
What's Not Good
Your Not Alone
Never Should

Letting Go
Is For The Best
On Your Own
The Greatest Test

Holding On To The Past
Can Only Bring Grief
Misery Will Last
Nothing To Achieve

Now Move On
Take The First Step
Your Not Alone
Just Don't Fret

Life

Life unfolds in many ways
Whether it's love or pain
Things are never the same
May even drive you insane

We live a life of mystery
Things of the unknown
The way it has to be
So life has shown

Some things remains to be seen
What you do to others
Like every human being
Don't even bother

Sometimes like a game
People always want to play
Then life is never the same
There is always a way

Don't put life on hold
Life passes by
Before we know it we're old
Don't ask why

Life Is

Life is a mystery
Broken dreams
Things aren't meant to be
Falling apart at the seems

Feeling so unhappy
Making you mad
Just not for me
Don't want to be sad

Life is a mystery
It's like a game
Just like history
Nothing's the same

All broken dreams
Just not living
What does it all mean
People not giving

Life is not the same
Things have changed
People play games
May drive you insane

Life Is Special

Life is special
In so many ways
Never guessing
Counting the days

Could be wonderful
Things you see
So I've been told
Sometimes hard to believe

How wonderful life can be
Like flowers or trees
It's a wonder to me
So much to see

So live it while you can
Life is special
Have a better plan
Make it the best

Always think ahead
Counting the days
What's been said
So many ways

Life Unfolds

Life's Unexpected Ways
Life Unfolds
What More Can I Say
It's The Way It Goes
Secrets Unravel
Life Unfolds
Sometimes It's A Battle
So The Story Is Told
Not Knowing Who's Your Friend
Life Unfolds
Even To The End
You Find Your On Own
Stolen Dreams
Life Unfolds
What Does It Mean
Everything's On Hold

Life's a Puzzle

Life's A Puzzle
Every time I Turn Around
In Everyway
Someone Tries To Bring Me Down

Always Going Through A Crowd
You'll Always Go Through A Maze
Never Feeling Proud
You Can Get So Crazed

When Things Go Your Way
They Only Bring You Down
Something Happening Today
Always Makes You Frown

Life's A Puzzle
But Never Fear
When you Use Your Head
Get Yourself In Gear
Get Off That Bed

Don't Let It Get In Your Way
Go With What's In Your Heart
Be Ready For Today
Cause Here It All Starts

Listen

Just Listen You'll Hear
What Life's Offering
You Won't Have To Fear
Don't Think It's Nothing

Listen And You'll See
Life Offers Many Things
You'll Be Able To Live Your Dream
Just Get Into The Swing

Listen To What's In Your Heart
Maybe You Will See
That This Is Just The Start
Some Things Aren't Meant To Be

Listen To Your Heart
You'll Live Life Freely
Now That's Smart
Then Come See Me

Listen Too What Life's Offering
You'll Have Plenty
Just Look And See
It Was Meant To Be

Living a Lie

Living A Life
I Thought Was Fine
Little Did I Know
I Was Living A Lie

You Came Into My Life
Thought It Was Fine
Everything Was So Nice
Feels As Though Your Mine

When You Confessed
It Goes To Show
You Wore Another's Dress
How Little Did I Know

Your Not Who I Thought You'd Be
A Life Full Of Happy Things
A Man Who Promised Me
Not Knowing What You'd Bring

Living A Life I Thought
Was Fine Little Did I Know
Misery Is What You've Brought
When It All Started To Show

I Was Living A Lie
Things You've Promised Me
Got To Live My Life
Wasn't Meant To Be

Look At

Look At That Man
He Looks So Sad
Over There Can
Make You Feel Sad

Look At That Lady
Over There
Just Maybe
Full Of Tears

It Seems No One Cares
What's This Come Too
No One Dares
Wants To Be There

The World Of The Nineties
They Don't Know What To Say
Look And Stare
Just Turn Away

Take A Good Look Around
Does Anyone Care
Look At
That Man Over There

"Look At"
People Today
What's That
They Say
Where You're At

Lost Hope

Gave Up On My Dreams
Don't Know What To Believe
Felt Like I Want To Die
Still Asking Why
Can't Just Close My Eyes

Oh How I Feel The Pain
Want Go Insane
Lost All My Dreams
Nothing Left To Believe
My Life Seems Like A Game

Living Life In Fear
Better Get In Gear
You'll Soon Find Your Alone
No One Really Cares
Is Anyone Out There

Feels Like I lost Hope
Don't Know If I Can Cope
Anymore With This Pain
It'll Drive Me Insane

Love's

Love's Not Fear
Love's When You Care
Love's Something You Share

Love's Not To Be Sold
Love's Not Control
Love's Till Your Old

Love's Trust
Love's Not Just Lust
Love's A Must

Love's When You Believe
Love's Something We All Need
Love's When Your Free

Love's Sometimes Funny
Love's When Life Seems More Sunny
Love's Having Joy Like A Bunny

Love's Bitter Sweet
Love's Like Having A Treat
Love's When One Heart Beats

Never Enough

It's Never Enough
No Matter What I Do
It's So Tough
Being With You

It's Never Enough
Never Satisfied
It's So Tough
What About Tonight

Not Even My Love
Can Keep It Alive
It's Never Enough
We Shall Say Goodbye

Can't Change Me
Take Me As I am
Wasn't Meant To Be
Only Way You Can

It's So Tough
Being With You
It's Never Enough
What I Do

Just have to Let Go
Got To Be Free
There Still Be Tomorrow
The Way It's Got To Be

No Sacrifice

Is it worth the sacrifice?
Giving up your life
When you know it isn't right
They're not very nice

Just don't care
Life's so unfair
When no one's there
Someone who can share

No sacrifice
Is worth giving up life
Just think twice
Don't want to die

Start living tonight
No sacrifice
It isn't right
Live your life

No sacrifice
Is worth your life
Think Twice
The future can be bright

Nothing Left

Nothing Left To See
Don't Know What To Believe
Feel So Lost And All Alone
Leaves Me Feeling Cold

When I Close My Eyes
I Always Want To Cry
Holding Back My Fears
Here Come Those Tears

Feel So Empty Inside
I Just Want to Die
Tired Of All The Lies
I Need Much More In Life

Nothing Left But To Cry
Can't You See The Tears In My Eyes
So Lost And All Alone
Don't Want to Go Home

Nothing's Real

Nothing seems real
In my world
Don't even want to feel
Not even diamonds and pearls

Slowly slipping away
Nothing's real
Do you hear what I am saying
Nothing left to feel

So empty inside
Just slipping away
Want to just hide
Nothing matters today

Feel so alone
Nothing seems real
Like the Twilight Zone
Nothing left to feel

Apart of me has died
Nothings real
So empty inside
Nothing to feel

Our Great Team

Army, Navy, Marines
Their a Great Team
Helping Others To Be Free
It's Part Of The Dream

From The Very Start
Time Of Ground Zero
Always In Our Hearts
They'll Be Our Hero's

You've Chose To Be Strong
Always Up For A Challenge
Showing You Belong
Don't Know How You Manage
Keeping Others Safe
Feeling Of Being Free
Even Today
Part Of The Dream

Air Force In the Air
Army, Navy, Marines
Never Despair
Our Great Team

Our Hero

Your our Hero
You've Sacrificed
A Day In Your Life
Never Thinking Twice

Your Our Hero
In Every Way
Not Just Robert De Niro
Children Can Play

You give us Hope
It feels More Safe
Gave Us Reason To Cope
There is A Better Way

You've Let others See
Now We All Know
There's A Hero in You and Me
Caring is What You've Shown

Love is Better Than Hate
Your Our Hero
In Every Way
It's Never Too Late

Peace, Not War

Looking At Life Go By
Is This Life
Isn't Very Nice

Don't Want to Die
Make Peace Not War
Want to Live Life
Got A Future In Store

So Many Faces
Haven't Seen
Got Many Places
Haven't Been

You Can't Take That From Me
Don't Want to Die
Wasn't Meant To Be
So Much More To Life

Make Peace Not War
We All Need Love
Life Has So Much More
We've Had Enough

Saying Goodbye

To My Father (Dimitros James Belias)

Here Today
Gone Tomorrow
A Better Way
Let Go Of The Sorrow
No Longer In Pain
His Spirit's Free
Never Is The Same
The Way It Should Be
Oh Father Please
Saying Goodbye
Set Him Free
Please Don't Cry
May He Rest In Peace
No more Suffering
The Way It should Be
What Life Brings
Saying Goodbye
Set Him Free
Please Don't Cry
The Way It Has To Be

Shame of Crime

Shame Of Crime
We Feel The Terror Inside
All Look Away Each Time
People Choose To Be Blind

Shame Of Crime Is Here
Makes You Want to Hide
Look At Them Over There
We Don't Know Why

Don't See What They're Doing
To You And Me
All The Shooting
We're Never Free

Is Right Before Our Eyes
Here In Our Time
Thought We Could Hide
Don't Be Blind

Stand Up For What You Believe
Use Our Minds
We All Can Achieve
Let's Beat It This Time

Sometimes

Sometimes got to let things be
Never Know what Tomorrow Brings
Life is a Mystery
With so Many Things
Sometimes I just can't see
What's in front of me
Feelings I'm Hiding
Can't no Longer Pretend
Don't Want it To End
May Have To Let It Go
Sometimes Got To Let things Be
But Then You'll Never Know
It'll Be a Mystery
Don't Know What's Happening
Sometimes Just Can't See
Just so Many Things
Is this Meant To Be
It's All A Mystery
Not Knowing What Life Brings
Just Can't See

Sometimes Goodbye

Sometimes have to say goodbye
When you know it isn't right
Don't ask why
Have to live my life

Sometimes have to let go
Things aren't always meant to be
It only goes to show
Someday you'll see

It's only a fantasy
You were just a dream
Not the one for me
Not what it seems

Sometimes saying goodbye
Is the only way
Starting a new life
Maybe someday

Another time and place
Have to let go
Give me space
In time you'll know

Tears

Don't think I could hide
The tears from within
It would be a lie
Don't know where to begin

How much it hurts
Knowing you'll be going
Just want to burst
Never knowing

The tears I hide
Trying not to look at your eyes
Can't say goodbye
Baby I want to cry

Just can't pretend
Feelings are real
Hope it don't end
The way I feel

Don't know where to begin
No need for me to lie
Tears come from within
Just can't hide

Feel like I want to cry
Can't say goodbye
No matter how hard I try
Tears start falling from my eyes

Time of Sorrow (Male Version)

"For Those Who've Lost"

In This Time Of Sorrow
We Grieve The One We Lost
Though It's Hard to Believe
He'll Soon Be In Peace

With Those he's Loved
Although he's Not Here
Her Spirit Remains
He'll Be Up Above

Someone We Trust
Can Hope And Pray
They'll Get Through This Pain
It Will Get Better Someday

Time of Sorrow (Female Version)
"For Those Who've Lost"

In This Time Of Sorrow
We Grieve The One We Lost
Though It's Hard to Believe
She'll Soon Be In Peace

With Those She's Loved
Although She's Not Here
Her Spirit Remains
She'll Be Up Above

Someone We Trust
Can Hope And Pray
They'll Get Through This Pain
It Will Get Better Someday

Tired

Tired of all this pain
Feels like I'm going insane
Nothing's to gain
Stop the blame

You've caused too much pain
Feel so lost inside
Nothing's the same
Can't no longer hide

Can't even cry
So much pain inside
My tears are all dry
Tired of all the lies

Just want to die
Tired of the pain
All this pain inside
Never going to be the same

Does anyone give a dam
Seems so cold and empty
Don't know who I am
Nothing to tempt me

United as One

In This Day And Age
Never Thought We'd See This Day
Just Like The Turning Of A Page
All Sadness On Our Face

Pain In Our Hearts
Twin Towers Are Gone
Tearing People Apart
We Will Go On

Though We All Grieve
We Unite As One
As You All Can See
We Still Stand Strong

Many Families Who Have Lost
With Tears In Their Eyes
Taking Lives At Any Cost
Still So Hard Too Believe

How Evil Some Can Be
Took Many So Innocent
Feels Like A Hole In Me
Nothing Really Makes Sense

Firefighters Oh So Brave
Police Officers Make It Safe
Proud To Be Born And Raised
New York A Greater Place

Coming Together As One
For All Too See
We Must Stand Strong
Just Like In My Dreams

What a Difference

What a difference does it make
When there's so much hate
They all want to just take
It's just too late

There's just too much hate
Just not living
So much has been taken
No more giving

What a difference does it make
When there's too much hate
Not much more I can take
Just too late

Life is never the same
Want it to end
Stop all the blame
My heart won't mend

All the hurt and pain
Nothings the same
No more to gain
Seems like a game

Where Are

Dreams aren't what they seem
Doesn't feel like living
Makes me want to scream
It's all broken

Tired of giving
Always hoping
Seems like nothing
Never knowing

Where are we going
There's no answer
Just not showing
Life just goes faster

Life is always changing
Never knowing
What life is bringing
Where are we going

It's all broken
Sometimes falling apart
We keep hoping
From the Start

Where to Begin

To many things going on
Don't know where to begin
Just want to be left alone
Feels like a world wind

Feels like a bad dream
Coming to an end
So it all seems
Will I see you again?

Happening to fast
Don't know where to begin
Wondering if it'll last
Can never win

Is it coming to an end
Will it last
Like a world wind
Going so fast

Want to be left alone
Where to begin
Let it all go
Could never win

Who's to Blame

Look At That Mark
On Her Face
That's When We're Left In The Dark
Seems Out Of Place

Who Can Explain The Anger
Who Can Explain The Rage
Nothing Seems To Change
You Take The Blame

"Who's To Blame"
When You See Her Cry
Everything's Locked Inside
When There's A Black Eye
Still Trying To Hide

Isn't It A Dam Shame
Always Being Accused
You Know That's Nothing New
It's A Part Of His Game

Don't Let Him Drive You Insane
Get Out Of That Place
You're Not To Blame
So Much Disgrace

You Can Make It On Your Own
Don't Be A Shamed
It's Ok To Be Alone
Things Start To Change

Why Suffer

"Those Who have Suffered"

Why should We Suffer
In the hands of another
You don't love her
Just like our Mother

Relieving our Fears
Just want to be Loved
Wondering if anyone Cares
But not this Way

Need to Get Away
Yet We Always Stay
Don't Understand Why
We Must Take The Pain

Nothing to Gain
Why Must We Suffer
In the HANDS of Another
Why Must We Suffer

Just going let It Go
Start To SAY NO!

With Life

With life
You never know
It could be nice
If you let go

One door opens
Another closes
Keep's you hoping
It's what life shows us

With life
It's a mystery
May have to think twice
You just can't see

Isn't always what it seems
Life's a mystery
Falling apart at the seems
Don't know what it means

With life
You can be happy
Can be nice
It's up to me

As one door opens
Now I can see
Keeps me hoping
Life is better for me

Printed in the United States
51527LVS00006B/928

9 781424 116539